Eric

"Enjoy"

J. B.

Glances of Life
Select Poems

J.B. Anderson
Illustrations by Maria Rodriguez

© 2017 J.B. Anderson

All Rights Reserved.

No part of this publication may be reproduced, stored in a retrieval system, or transmitted, in any form or by any means, electronic, mechanical, photocopying, recording, or otherwise, without the written permission of the author.

First published by Dog Ear Publishing
4011 Vincennes Rd
Indianapolis, IN 46268
www.dogearpublishing.net

ISBN: 978-1-4575-5615-9

This book is printed on acid-free paper.

Printed in the United States of America

DEDICATION

*Special thanks to my wife Mary Beth,
to Maria Rodriguez and to all of my muses..........*

TABLE OF CONTENTS

I. INTRIGUE

First Glance 1

Shattered 3

IT 5

Monotony 7

Does it Matter? 9

Butterfly Dance 11

Foxglove 13

The Race 15

Entanglements - A Prayer 17

Transformation 19

Good Friday on the Via Dolorosa 21

Augury 23

II. WHIMSY

Birthday Mitt 27

Fungi 29

Martins at 9 O'clock 31

The Bump 33

Showtime 35

Whistle   37

Third Grade Bee FF   39

What is it Like?   41

The Kitten and the Bee   43

Greenhorn   45

Chasing Butterflies   47

III. REFLECTION

The Talisman   51

How Do You Talk to a Butterfly?   53

i   55

That   57

Dilemma   59

Dusk   61

Last Fly   63

Faces   65

Pas de Deux   67

Private Showing   69

The Day After   71

The Meeting   73

I.
INTRIGUE

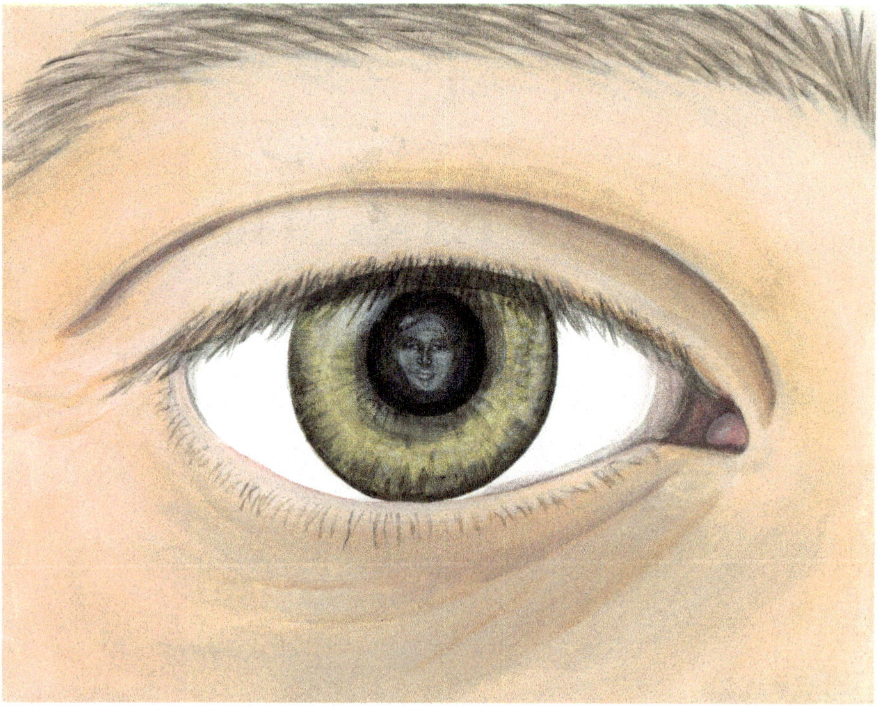

FIRST GLANCE

Inananosecond
The photons reflect
From your face and zip
Through the lens of my eye -
Your image summersaults on my retina
Where all comes into brilliant sharp focus
Then the rhodopsin in the colorful cones
And sensitive rods transforms to create
The impulse which crosses
Via the optic chiasm
To the visual cortex
Where all is parsed -
And though I have
Never seen you
In the past
Somehow
I know
You are
Beautiful

SHATTERED

Mirror, Mirror on the wall
Who is the fairest of them all?

The irate queen as we know -
Learned it was a girl named Snow

Then she decreed through tough tears
There would be no more mirrors

To further wreck their morale
She banned everything digital

Apples fell and Canons burst
Wrinkle creams suffered worse

Plastic surgeons had no work
Movie stars went berserk

Only cats and dogs were blase'
Mirrors were just in their way

Soon the pall began to lift
As the sybarites went adrift

Even though they were unkempt
Finally all could now attempt

To give each other a true look
Instead of through a worn Facebook

IT

IT controls our modern life but
IT really does not care if
IT slows things down because
IT speaks only in digITal so
IT does not see nuance nor does
IT ever have a heart hence
IT goes along its speedy way
(IThinking?)
IT is our savior when really
IT just tears down our beliefs -
IT should know that someday
IT will be the end of IT

MONOTONY

Listen to the frenetic mockingbird mock my mediocrity
And my rut 'round middle C. Even though its constant
Coloratura is sublime, does it wonder, as vanilla I do,
If it should be, not gray, but perhaps red robed like the cardinal
Or in black tuxedo like the tenor who struts the stage?
Like me, does it tire of endless miming and strive to change
The *idée fixe* and break the chain of life's plain chant?

DOES IT MATTER?

The frizzycists say
In their particular way
Everything boils down
To forces and waves

To make matter better
They discovered
The boson of Higgs which
Breaks down the "symmetry"

Now the forces of nature
Are clearer than ever
Or that is what they
Would have us believe

Are they just stringing
Us along like
A meandering neutrino
Or perhaps a lost photon

For me I'd rather hear
The sweet song of a Lark -
They can have their
Up and down quarks

And when it comes to forces
I prefer the smack of a kiss
Or the tight squeeze of a hug -
The things which attract you to me

BUTTERFLY DANCE

Two small butterflies dance in the sun
Aero-acrobatics twist into one

Alabaster wings waltz to a three-four beat
Next a sultry samba rises with the heat

Hit stall speed in blue yonder sublime
Tango on down with wings intertwined

Finish with snap rolls - give it some flair
Tempo is up as they jive in thin air

I still can can see them though they are gone
Oh how I miss those pretty *papillons*

FOXGLOVE

Hiding head down in your lavender lair
Surrounded by your guardians
The prickly blackberries
And the flourishing fuchsia

Will you lift up your eyes once again
To pedal your powerful nostrum
Which made my heart pound
With the force of a young buck

I realized later it was
That sudden bitter aftertaste
Which almost brought me
To my demise - Dare I try again?

THE RACE

Stroke yells the coxswain when the gun fires
And every tendon, nerve and muscle fiber
Is alive as the eight oars simultaneously
Caress the river without a sound or a splash

Stroke - Always struggling to find the perfect one -
To swim like a butterfly, to make the easy ace

Stroke - The tresses of her hair when love
Is in the air

Stroke - How often it is a lucky one which
Changes life so fast

Stroke - Amazing how a gentle one is all
Your favorite pet demands

Stroke - The mighty pen rules within the law
Or steals our liberties

Stroke - Now every sinew aches
As we near the finish line

Stroke - it is midnight - BEWARE

ENTANGLEMENTS - A PRAYER

I could never unfigure it out

The sneaky snaky garden hose
Somehow knows how to twist
And turn itself askew
So there is nary a drop
When I turn it on

Or the devilish orange electric cord
No matter the pains I take
To keep it straight
It ravels like Rastafarian locks
As I try to trim the lawn

Even those affairs of men
Which start out simple
So it seems
Become a thick burgoo
Which sucks the mighty down

So my request to you dear Lord -
Please do undo all this men*angst*tal
Before it undoes us all

meAn

TRANSFORMATION

It started when I bought
An art deco Neon Green bracelet
At Ye Olde Antique Shop
And then I tried it on

Well, it looked a little clunky
But I wore it to the market
Where I saw this buxom blonde
In a Neon Green chiffon dress

She was in the produce aisle
Selecting unripe bananas
I admired her *savoir-faire*
Amidst the conventional throng

I kept her image as I entered
My slate-gray Dodge Neon
Where in the center of the windshield
Was a sublime Neon Green insect

It remained fixed in my view
As I drove slowly away
Knowing it was going
To be fun to be Neon Green

GOOD FRIDAY ON THE VIA DOLOROSA

Scum!

Another one of those Pharisees dragging
His bloody cross
Doesn't Pontius Pilate know how this interferes
With our shops
On this, the busiest day of the week?

Look at this one   They say He is a Messiah   My
Such sunken downcast eyes
And why are all these weeping wenches
Following Him?
Don't they have anything better to do?
Sweep? Scrub? Cook?

Why don't the Romans just flog these Nezers
Where they try them?
Why do they have to go all the way up the hill
Just to be crucified?
After all, we pay good taxes to keep riffraff
Off our streets

Disgusting!

AUGURY

When
Hecate displays
A full crimson moon
On two successive evenings
It must portend certain
Cosmic responses
The mystery
Is always
Where?

Who
Would appear
The very next day
Soft on my window pane
With saffron speckled wings
Conjuring her flaxen hair
The only question
Remaining is
Why?

II.
WHIMSY

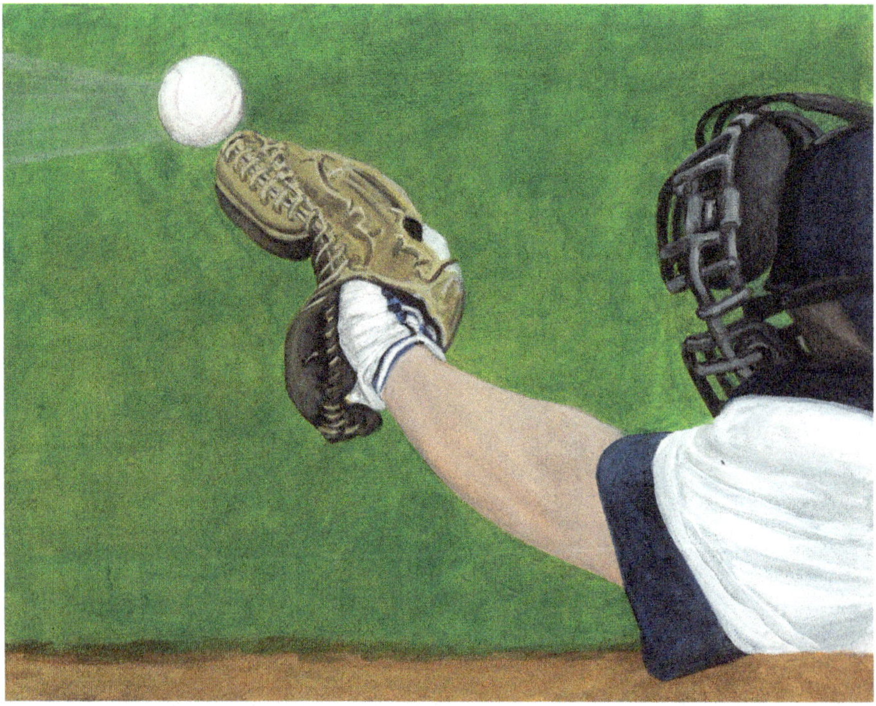

BIRTHDAY MITT

"Are you ready?"

His first two offerings
Were nothing -
Just soft lobs to help
Break in the pocket

I donned my mask, kicked
Each shin guard, adjusted
My imaginary cup - crouching low
I gave him a knee high target

The new leather smell of the mitt
Sharpened my senses
As I wiggled my index finger
To call for all of his speed

His windup was smoooth

That is all I remember
Except for the fast whirr
And the slight tick
On the top of the mitt

Gasping, I went down
In a heap
As the ball struck
The plexus of my soul

Now I was ready

FUNGI

I was a lonely fungi
Ensconced between some toes
But then I met Miss Dezi Nex
Well - You know how it goes

She blew some powder over me
To lure me from my haunt
But I was not impressed
With such a tepid taunt

Then she tried an aerosol
It really was a blast
But despite all the shock and awe
I managed to hold on fast

She finally used an ointment,
Unctuous Mr. Nizarol,
Who slid me from my lair
And caused my final fall

Dezi and I will marry soon
In a dark and obscure crease
The combination of this
I hope will, at least, yield yeast

MARTINS AT 9 O'CLOCK

My yellow panzer roared through
The high grass - blades whirling
General Rommel would be proud
The way I drove her like a slick Mercedes

From out of the morning sun
Three purple blue martins swooped
Down on me at full throttle
In tight textbook formation

Diving, twisting, turning they came
As one - then split and chandelled
Behind me and as I turned to find them
They returned with even more dash

Now I was their supreme ally
In this feeding frenzy - the tracers
Of mosquitoes, moths and gnats
Whirled up in a tumultuous flurry

But our battle formation pursued
Its prey with a perfect harmony
Of ground and air power - we overwhelmed
Them with our relentless assault

I saluted the trio as they performed
Several triumphant snap rolls and hurtled
Into the heavens with a dip of their wings
My blue angels were sated!

THE BUMP

My little donkey Rosie
Has a bump on her nose
I suppose I must efface
This bump before it further grows

First I called a phrenologist
Whose specialty is bumps
He took one look at Rosie
And said "Yes, that's quite a lump"

So! - I called a dermatologist
Who knows all about the skin
She took a biopsy of the bump
To find what there was within

The biopsy was benign
Which made things very simple
I called the local thaumaturgist
To change the bump into a dimple

He laid his hands on Rosie's nose
And mumbled a cryptic spell
This caused a cloud of awful smoke
And a result I have to tell

I think he got it bassakwards
Although Rosie doesn't care
'Cause now her nose is smooth as glass
But the bump's on her derriere

SHOWTIME

Her Grace and I settle into our seats
She next to her scratch post
I deep in my recliner to watch
As Nature raises the curtain of clouds
Halfway up from the horizon to reveal
Earth's final degrees of rotation for this day

Brilliant vermillion splashes appear in the curtain
But are diluted to orange and lavender
Before sinking into a layered kaleidoscope
In the azure below; overwhelmed
The blue asserts itself with streaks of varied gray
While the sun holds fast as a gold sliver

With the ebb of the sun, the colors anneal
And transform - oranges become rust;
Mauves - deep purple; grays - infinite black

The relentless rotation slowly silhouettes
Two leafless trees in the distance which signify
            "The End"

A single credit rolls down the screen
As we exit into the night

WHISTLE

I have a dear younger sister
Who has the best wolf whistle whistle
She puts two fingers in her mouth
And emits a sound as clear as crystal

Since I am male and inventive
I know deep within my heart
There must be a way to fathom
How she mastered this manly art

But no matter how much I huff
And puff and blow 'til I am red -
The only noise which comes from me
Sounds as if it came from the dead

So as a last resort I have prayed
To those gods on high who whistle
And they promptly sent to me
A package via UPS missile

The payload was red blue and white
And when I opened it I realized
That within its aromatic packing
There was a great surprise -

Now I am grown up and I work
As a basketball official
I deftly control all the games
With my plastic Cracker Jack whistle

THIRD GRADE BEE FF

The first three words were the
Usual fluff - dog, stop, park

The next one was a real kerfuffle!

Should I write it on my hand?
Ask for the language of origin?

But I was never one to waffle

So, I began:
   "e" that was easy
   "n" not too bad
   hmm - "u"?
   how about "f"??
   and why not another "f"???

The bell went ding -
I sat down in a huff

To this day
That word is just too tuff!

WHAT IS IT LIKE?

What is it like to have a tail?
Which flips and flops behind your back
And keeps your balance when you run
Use it to tease a playful male

What is it like to be a snail?
To take a month to travel a mile
And have your own house on your back
To get your mail, leave a slime trail

What is it like to be a nail?
To have a hammer pound your head
'Til your neck bends ninety degrees
Don't lean on <u>that</u> rickety rail

What is it like to be a sail?
To catch the wind along the mast
Better to be taut, rather than limp
Unless, off course, you're in a gale

What is it like to be a whale?
To be the kingpin of the sea
Only the sharks dare come too close
Everyone knows they read by Braille

What is it like to never fail?
To go through life without a flaw
And never learn from your mistakes
Ever behind your opaque veil

Now I think I must end this tale
Of silly rhymes and deep nonsense
It seems I've run out of words
Which sparkle like pale ginger ale

THE KITTEN AND THE BEE

The bee's languid loops
Arouse
The napping kitten

One perfect soft right hook
And the bee is down

Downside up
It spins like
A toddler's toy

Now it is a soccer ball
Dribbled on rough cement

It rights itself
But weighty wings
No longer give it flight

And once potent stinger
Serves as no defense

One final playful pounce
And the warning
Buzz is gone

GREENHORN

His huge brown eye scans me as I approach
Him from the side
I stroke his live hard neck to soothe
His fears as well as mine

Shaking I slip
The fly mask over his ears
I smooth back his forelock then snap
The double Velcro strap secure

He seems to acquiesce a moment while I place
His halter overhead and lead
Him to the paddock gate which groans
And clanks to open grudgingly

Though now I cannot see those huge brown eyes
To know if they are pleased
As I release the lead he gives a kick fart snort
And races pell mell into his pasture green

CHASING BUTTERFLIES

Chasing butterflies is a delicate art

One must be quick and sly
And expect to gather
Lots of air

Lucky for me I started
The Pursuit when
I was three or was it four?

I never used a net
It was against my rules
I thought it was not fair

So through the years I pursued
Large and small with colors galore
But success was never there

Running up a hill one day
I came upon a rabble:
Yellow ones with one white spot

Like bursts of sun they spread their joy
And as I turned among them
I caught one magically

I felt its frantic flutter -
So I opened my hands
And set it free!

III.
REFLECTION

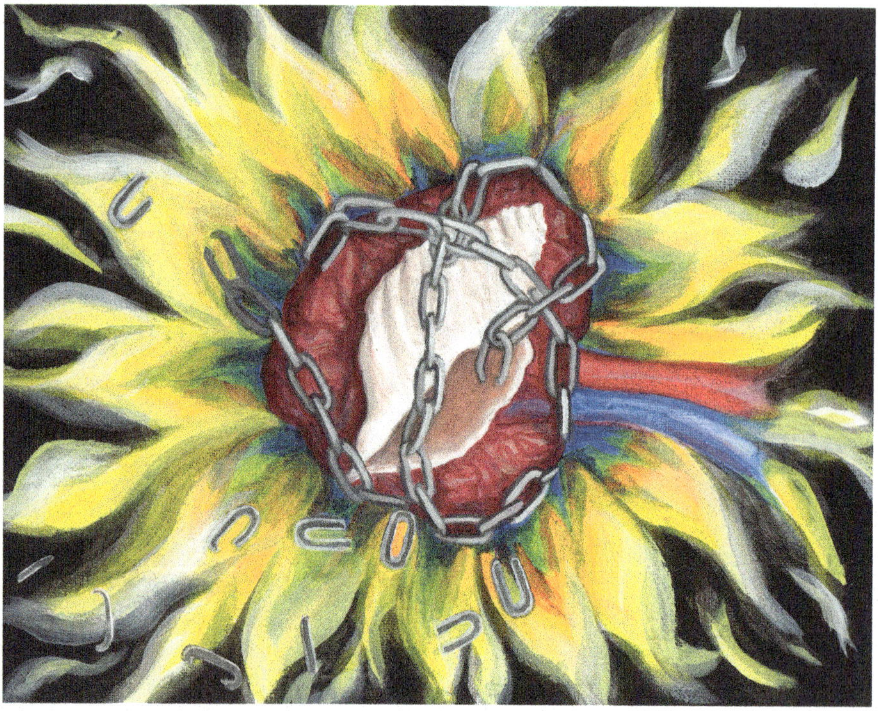

THE TALISMAN

She thought she found the perfect shell
Along the crowded, noisome shore -
But only time would really tell

At first is seemed to cast a spell
When it around her neck she wore
She thought she found the perfect shell

But as the days ran pell mell
Questions began to prick her core -
But only time would really tell

Then someone would her doubt dispel
And once again her heart would soar
She thought she found the perfect shell

In vain she even tried to expel
This shell she once did adore
But only time would really tell

At last in her death knell
She unchained this thing she did abhor
Still - she thought she found the perfect shell
But often - time is really hell

HOW DO YOU TALK WITH A BUTTERFLY?

How do you talk with a butterfly?
By chance, I found out yesterday

I see the same butterfly each day
Each day she wears different attire

She may present in faded jean blue
Or solid ebon with gold lace

Yesterday she was in brilliant sun yellow
To attract my eye to her

She landed horizontal on my window sill
And waited patiently

Then as if pulling on a thin thread she tapped out
A strange code with her wings

Seeing I was puzzled she fluttered to my shoulder
And whispered in my ear

"Rendezvous with me tomorrow
Near the flower called Linnea

Be alert - I will be camouflaged
Among its petals"

With that she hovered before my eyes
Then she disappeared

How do you talk with a butterfly?
Fly with me and I'll show you the way!

i

Imagine a number, we'll call it *i*
They say it's as easy as π in the sky

If you rotate your brain 90 degrees
Certainly *i* becomes more clear

Now let's muddle it up and add a real number
To make things really complex

Throw in Euler's number *e* and voila!
You have a mathematical brew

When all is prepared you can relax
And enjoy the brew with a real piece of pie

For your next task why not attempt
Something simple like the concept of God

Which thankfully for your strained brain
Has neither an *e* nor an *i*

THAT

If that is anathema
To you, and you insist that
We never endeavor to use
That with a bland word like flat

How can we poets that strain
Every inch of our brain
Ever fill up that blank page
That stares at us *sans merci*?

That that could be so maligned
When with only three letters
That quite often unfetters
Any poor reason or rhyme

DILEMMA

Kant - can't one
Ever tell a lie?
Never?

Herr Professor I realize
You never married
So you would never know

How the husbands
Of this world
Are always in a bind

When their wives
Pose those questions
Which make our minds unwind

They ask us if we like
The new do - or if we think
Their dress is too tight

Now how is one
To answer without
Provoking a fractious fight

Of course, I submit
You would opine
Those questions are rhetorical

We husbands should
Just keep mum before
Things become hysterical

Cogito ergo to sum it up
Concerning lying:
One really never - Kant

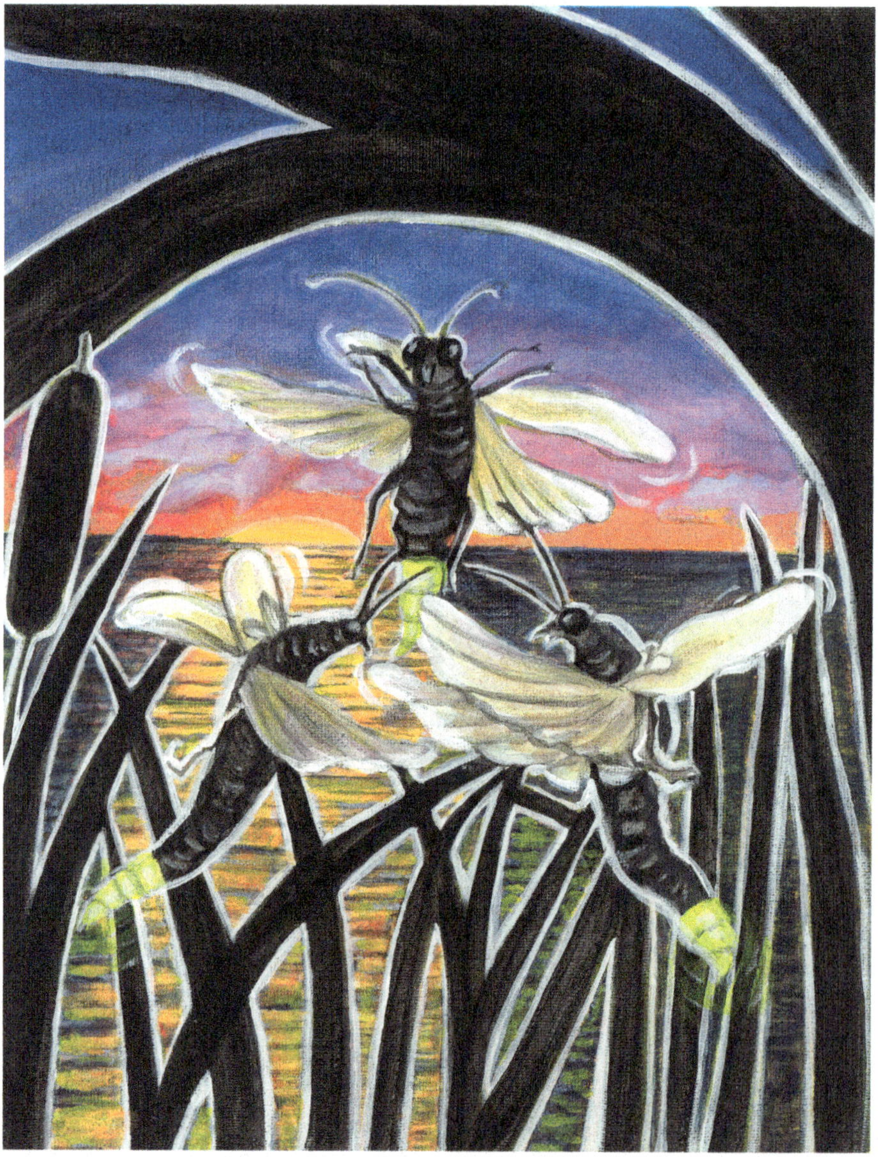

DUSK

As the stiletto shaped cloud
Slices
The setting sun
Spewing
Its lavender and crimson
Rays
Into the horizon below

The fireflies
Dance
To this orgy of last light
Igniting
Their passionate
Glow
To lure a mate for the night

LAST FLY

The last fly of fall circles
Haphazardly interrupting
My pre-dawn read

A magazine is folded
And ready to swat
Its final buzz away

But the dizzy moribund
Flight eludes
My futile flails

As it makes a languid loop
Into the light to seek
Its natural demise

FACES

If I could turn every dream
Into pure reality
All will be changed at once
Like the quick twist of a key

My friends and loves will join me
Even those who left too soon
Our eyes will meet at a freckle
The time, of course, high noon

We will approach infinity
Beyond the farthest star
And then assemble here on earth
On this side of the bar

There will be no book of faces
No blogs, no texts, no tweets
Only face to face conversation
For all, the perfect sweets

Some will say it is a ruse
And cannot ever be
When I convert all my dreams
Into my new reality

PAS DE DEUX

Two majestic hawks
Float high upon
The afternoon thermals
Turning in tandem

So slow

The only sound is
The smooth whoosh
Under steady wings

Below - I smile -
Then pirouette
In honor of their recherché

They bow - then hie to the hunt

PRIVATE SHOWING

All I had to do
On that quiet
Christmas Eve morn
Was to finally turn
The corner - then
Throttle back

There were
No bands
No ads
No tailgaters
No rush
No crush

Diana appeared
Center stage
To flaunt
Her full silver pendant
    Suspended
By a thin wisp of clouds

I stayed to the end

    Attendance:
       1

THE DAY AFTER

No one talks about
The day after the battle
When the saber remains
Half-drawn in the scabbard

The colors lay tattered
And no one runs to raise them
Nor taps the drum nor blows
The bugle to lead the charge

Spiked cannons are silent
And caissons are tangled
With horses which never wanted
To be men of war

Victors and vanquished share
The blank stare captured
In photos on pages where
No one cares to pause

There is only one who reaps
The fodder of fools -
And he scatters it
Without a pause or a care

THE MEETING

I met God the other day -
She was serving eggamuffins and coffee
At the McDonalds on Route 278
All with a big bright smile

In spite of the hungry crowd
She seemed without hurry
And had several kind words
For each clamoring customer

Normally, I would have grabbed
My breakfast and been on my way
But curiosity made me
Relax and even enjoy my meal

As I departed, I noticed
She no longer had customers waiting
So I thought this was my chance
To ask Her for directions

In a meek voice I asked
If this was the correct route -
She placed her chubby black hand
On my shoulder and said:

Just go straight on this winding road -
You will be there in no time -
And oh, by the way, your friend
Is doing just fine *chez moi*

J.B. Anderson
(Author)

J.B. Anderson was born and raised in Detroit.

He graduated from the University of Michigan with a Bachelor of Arts in English literature.

He went on to attend the Wayne State University School of Medicine and practiced orthopedic surgery for thirty years.

His interests include swimming, skiing, music and poetry.

In 2010, he published a children's book *Hockey Cat* under the *nom de plume* Rollo J. Pondmarsh.

Presently, he lives in Armada, Michigan with his wife Mary Beth and their five cats - Stevie Y, Gracie, Splenda, Belle and Seven, and their Tennessee Walker, Cochise.

Maria Rodriguez
(Illustrator)

Maria Rodriguez, artist and mother of three resides in Grosse Pointe, Michigan. She has a BBA from Loyola University of Chicago with majors in marketing and art.

Maria exhibits her work in galleries throughout Michigan and the U.S.

Her company name is Creations of the Spirit. She creates book illustrations, murals and paintings on commission for both residential and commercial clients.

Maria's artwork has been published in the children's books *Belly Button Love* by Kelly Hagen, *Hockey Cat* by Rollo Pondmarsh, *Taste and See* by Rene Deachen.

Her illustrations have also been published in *La Voz Normal* by Christina Menaldi.

Her preferred medium is acrylics and oils. She paints trompe l'oeil murals, landscapes, portraits and canvases that are vibrantly colorful.

Her paintings can be seen at www.creationsofthespirit.com.

Maria has a passion for painting, design, photography, music, dance, yoga, animals, dark chocolate, kids, family and LOVE.

CPSIA information can be obtained
at www.ICGtesting.com
Printed in the USA
LVOW06*1932230617
539137LV00009B/24/P

9 781457 556159